The Clew Bay Archaeological Trail

Slí Seandálaíochta Chuan Módh

exploring 6,000 years of mayo's heritage

www.clewbaytrail.com

SUPPORTED BY

Mayo County Council

South West Mayo Development Company Ltd.

Comhdáil Oileáin na hÉireann
Irish Islands Federations

Welcome to Clew Bay

Page No.:

Contents

Foreword – Mayo County Council . . . 3
Introduction – Harry Hughes . . . 4
Exploring 6,000 Years of Mayo's Heritage . . . 5
Getting Around the Trail . . . 6
Putting Mayo's History in Context . . . 8
Weather – Always a Talking Point . . . 10

Stage I: Westport

	Clew Bay	14
1.	Clew Bay Heritage Centre	15
2.	Boheh Stone	16
3.	Carrownalurgan Ringfort	18
4.	Oughavale (Aughaval) Graveyard and Churches	20

Stage II: Murrisk

	Croagh Patrick	24
5.	Annagh-Killadangan Bronze Age Archaeological Complex	26
6.	Murrisk Abbey	28
7.	National Famine Monument	30
8.	Statue of St Patrick	31
9.	Glaspatrick Church	32

Stage III: Louisburgh

10.	Kilgeever Abbey	36
11.	Lime Kiln, Moneen	38
12.	Famine Museum and Granuaile Centre	39
13.	Altóir-Srahwee Megalithic Wedge Tomb	41
14.	Clapperbridge, Bunlahinch	42
15.	Killeen Graveyard and Cross Slab	44

Stage IV: Clare Island

	Clare Island	48
	Granuaile	49
16.	Clare Island Tower-house	51
17.	Clare Island Abbey	53
18.	Bronze Age Promontory Fort	55
19.	Signal Tower	56
20.	Megalithic Court Tomb	57
21.	Fulachta Fiadh	58

Clew Bay Archaeological Trail Committee . . . 59
Acknowledgements . . . 60
Photographs . . . 61

Foreword

Pl. 1 - The clock in Westport,
a starting point for walkings tours of the town.

This Archaeological Trail located in the natural amphitheatre of Clew Bay presents the visitor with a challenging yet fulfilling journey. Here the visitor is encouraged to pause and look back almost 6,000 years over a sacred landscape punctuated by tangible evidence of lives lived according to the turbulence of the time, be they pagan, enlightened or persecuted. These treasures have been entombed by indifference and the grinding battle for survival, preserved for a time where we can afford the luxury of interpreting them in a comprehensive yet unobtrusive manner. To know ourselves and to go forward with direction we must know the path we have been on already. This trail invites us to discover this winding path.

The subtlety and simplicity of the various sites belie their profound significance, located as they are in pastoral unadorned locations connected by this panoramic trail terminating appropriately on Clare Island – the key to Clew Bay. This trail, displaying timeless relics from the dawn of civilisation in Mayo to the recent past, bestows a perspective on local history in a clear and user-friendly way, making it accessible and understandable while protecting the environmental heritage.

This enlightened endeavour sparked by local initiative and with the full co-operation of the community is surely a shining example of the way partnership was meant to serve the people. Mayo County Council is proud to be associated with the Clew Bay Archaeological Trail and will provide every assistance in securing and promoting what will be a successful and educational venture.

Cllr. Frank Chambers,
Cathaoirleach, Mayo County Council,
July 2003.

Introduction

Pl. 2 - Clew Bay & Clare Island.

The Clew Bay Archaeological Trail takes you through the magnificent scenery around Clew Bay and its many islands, past majestic Croagh Patrick and onto tranquil Clare Island. Nature has been generous to the Clew Bay region. When you overlay 6,000 years of human habitation, you get a multitude of pre-Christian and early Christian archaeological sites. In the 1980s a mining company discovered gold in Croagh Patrick. However the Trail offers you another type of bullion, a rich heritage, a glorious environment and many golden beaches accredited with Blue Flag status. The Trail is complimented by this book, which is extensively researched and engagingly written by Edel Hackett.

Six local community groups have come together to give visitors an opportunity to visit this natural outdoor museum of archaeology, history and folklore. This has been made possible by the generosity of private landowners, local parish and public authorities, which have all supported this trail. The committee are particularly indebted to the South West Mayo Development Company, Comhdháil Oileáin na hÉireann and Mayo County Council for their financial support.

The slogan for Mayo Tourism is Mayo Naturally. The Clew Bay Archaeological Trail is Mayo at its most natural. We hope your journey is enlightening and that it gives you an appreciation of the archaeology, heritage and environment of the Clew Bay area.

Bronagh Joyce

Chairperson of the organising committee:

Clare Island Development Co., Louisburgh Community Council, Murrisk Development Association, Croagh Patrick Archaeological Committee, Westport Tourism, Westport Chamber of Commerce.

Exploring 6,000 Years of Mayo's Heritage

Welcome to Clew Bay, one of Ireland's most spectacular sea inlets, with its distinctive rounded islands and majestic Clare Island rising out of the sea at its mouth. You can't help but be impressed with your surroundings as you look across the bay.

But, look a little closer. In the landscape that surrounds Clew Bay, there is even more to marvel at than first meets the eye. People have lived, loved, farmed, fought, prayed, mourned and danced in this area for over 6,000 years. Fortunately for us, they have left vital traces of their lives behind them.

The Clew Bay Archaeological Trail gives you a chance to explore these important traces. Stretching a magical 35 km, it tells an intricate story of the relationship between this land and its people – how they might have farmed, how they worshipped and how they mourned their dead.

Pl. 3 - Caher Island.

Along the Trail, you can see rock art, which was carved as early as the pyramids were built in Egypt. You can visit one of the best examples of a megalithic tomb in the country or reflect on the thousands who perished in Mayo during the Great Famine of the 1840s. You can wander around the island home of Granuaile, the famous sea captain of the late 1500s, or you can wonder at the scientific knowledge of people, who, over 5,000 years ago, aligned standing stones with the setting sun during the winter's solstice over Croagh Patrick.

The Clew Bay Archaeological Trail gives you 6,000 years of Mayo's heritage in one afternoon.

Getting Around the Trail

Tailor-Make Your Visit

This trail stretches from Westport to south of Louisburgh and then out to Clare Island at the mouth of Clew Bay. Along the way, it takes in 21 archaeological and heritage sites.

That can be a lot to take in on one visit. Therefore, we have divided the Clew Bay Archaeological Trail into four distinct sections with natural stop-off or start-up points, so that you can tailor-make your own trail. You can choose to visit all 21 sites or you can concentrate on a select number of sites only.

You do not have to visit the sites in any chronological order or sequence, and you will not miss out on any vital pre-emptive information if you chose to visit just a few sites.

Guidebook and Maps

This guidebook provides you with a description of each of the sites on the Trail, including anecdotes, legends and social histories, helping to bring the story of Mayo's heritage alive. It gives you the Gaelic names for the site locations with a direct English translation of their meaning. In addition, it provides background information about the Clew Bay area. To help you get around the trail there are maps of the complete trail with directions to the next and previous sites.
Finally, you can explore our website at www.clewbaytrail.com

Distinctive Signposting

The Trail is well marked with distinctive signposts. All signposts bear the unique Clew Bay Archaeological Trail logo, seen here.

Fig. i - Clew Bay Archaeological Trail logo.

Care Along the Way

Many of the Trail sites are close to roadways. Please take care when parking and remember that traffic in Ireland travels on the left-hand side of the road. Always use the lay-by areas to park when provided.

In many cases along the Trail, you will have to leave the roadside and, in some cases, enter private land. Always respect the Country Code. *Take only pictures and leave only footprints.*

- Wear boots or good walking shoes.
- Close all gates and cross all fences and walls by either gates or stiles.
- Do not bring dogs on the trail.
- Do not disturb livestock or interfere with any machinery.
- Leave no litter.
- Protect wildlife and plants.
- Make no unnecessary noise.
- Do not leave your name or graffiti anywhere.

Want to Know More?

For further information about archaeology and heritage around Clew Bay, read:
Croagh Patrick: An Ancient Mountain Pilgrimage by Harry Hughes
Croagh Patrick, Co. Mayo - Archaeology, Landscape and People by Leo Morahan,
Antiquities of West Mayo by Christiaan Corlett.

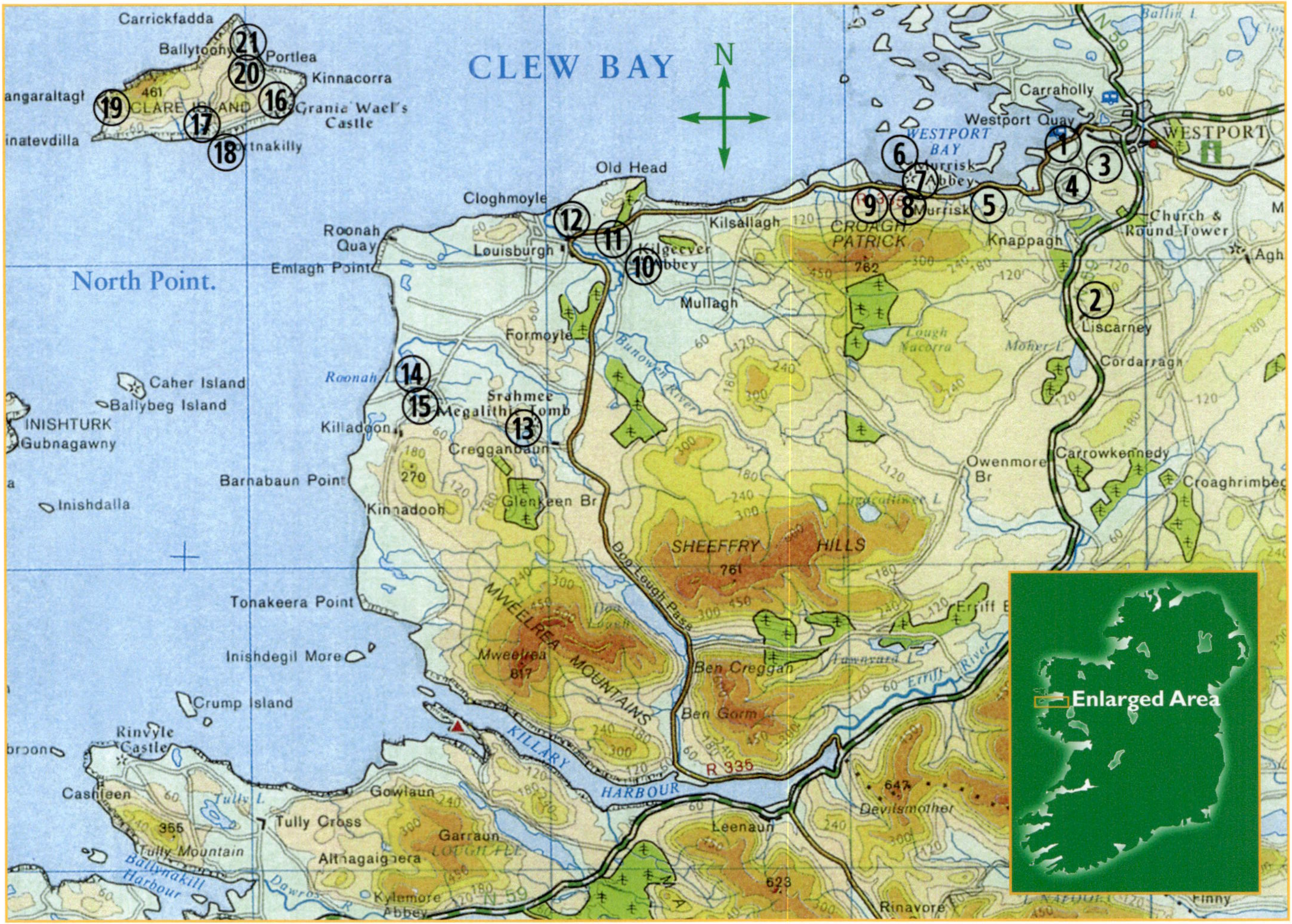

Fig. ii - Map of The Clew Bay Archaeological Trail.
Not to Scale - Permission granted for use from Ordnance Survey Ireland.

putting mayo's HISTORY IN CONTEXT . . .

Years	Age
4,000 BC	New Stone Age/ Neolithic
2,500 BC	Early Bronze Age
1,200 to 600 BC	Late Bronze Age/ Early Iron Age
600 BC to 400 AD	Iron Age
400 to 1,100 AD	Early Middle Ages/ Early Christianity
1,100 to 1,600	Late Middle Ages
1,600 – 1,900	The Modern Era

Mayo Events	Related Sites on the Trail	World Events
First Farming Court Tombs Pre-bog Walls Rock Art	Clare Island 20 Clare Island 2	First known wheel First Pyramids
Wedge Tombs Beginnings of Mining Early Gold and Jewellery Early Copper Axes	13	Stonehenge
Fulachta Fiadh Barrows – earth and burial mounds Hill Forts Swords, Arrows Standing Stones	21 Croagh Patrick 5	Halstatt Celts, Austria Beginnings of coinage in China, Greece, Italy
Celts in Ireland Crannógs Lake Forts Promontory Forts Black Pigs Dyke Na Fianna and other Legends	 Moher Lake (just past Site 2) 18	Greek and Roman Empires
Ireland christianised by St Patrick First Churches Cross Slabs Holy Wells Ringforts Vikings arrive in Clew Bay	Croagh Patrick 4, 8, 14 9, 14 4, 10 3	Irish settlement in West Britain and Iceland Birth of Mohammed
Normans in Ireland – founded Castlebar, Ballinrobe and Burrishoole Gaelic Revival under O'Malleys Tower Houses Abbeys	 Granuaile 16 6, 10, 17	Columbus discovers America Conquest of Central and South America The Incas, South America The Renaissance
Flight of the Earls (Wild Geese) Conquest by Cromwell Penal Laws Westport planned as Georgian Town Famine	 13 7, 10, 12, 20	First printing press French Revolution American Revolution

Weather – Always a Talking Point

If you spend any length of time in West Mayo, you will know that it is possible to experience four seasons in one day. You will also know that it is probably not possible to get through a day without some reference to the weather – greetings and chit chat are invariably accompanied by some comment on the prevailing rain, wind, clouds, and of course, sunshine.

Weather change affects people's lives on a daily basis around Clew Bay; but climate change over the longer term has had a profound influence on the way in which the area has developed physically and how the people who have lived here have adapted to those developments.

Mountains, Valleys and Islands

Croagh Patrick's quartzite peak was formed some 410-440 million years ago. At that it is the new kid on the block. The Nephin Beg mountain range on the north side of Clew Bay was formed 600-750 million years ago and the Sheeffry Hills, south of Louisburgh, were formed between 440 and 510 million years ago.

Pl. 4 - There were two glaciers on Croagh Patrick.

These mountains were originally large plateaus, but were broken up by faulting and fracturing caused by the movements of the earth's crust. The last Ice Age, beginning about 18,000 years ago, saw the formation of huge glaciers in these mountains, sculpting steep sided valleys and lakes. There were two glaciers on Croagh Patrick, the remains of which are seen as a corrie lake on the northern side of the mountain.

The ice sheets from these mountain ranges met on the flat land between Westport and Newport. With movement, the ice sheets gouged out holes in the land below and then dumped and shaped their cargo as rounded hills, or drumlins. With increasing temperatures, the ice sheets receded and much of this flat area became flooded by the sea, thus creating Clew Bay, where the drumlins now appear as the bay's distinctive islands.

The First People

The ice sheets retreated finally around 10,000 years ago and earliest known evidence indicates that Ireland's first human visitors arrived about 9,000 years ago, during the Middle Stone Age. The Ireland they encountered was densely covered in forests of oak, hazel, pine, elm and ash. They were hunters, fishers and gatherers, living off the fruits and nuts of the forest, wild animals and birds, as well as salmon and eels. They had no concept of farming or settlement and moved around the country to ensure a continuous supply of food.

Because these nomadic people left very little trace of settlement behind, it is difficult to identify their presence in the Mayo area, except for finds at Castlebar Lakes, Urlaur and Burrishoole.

There is more tangible evidence of human occupation around Clew Bay from about 6,000 years ago, or during the New Stone Age, due primarily to the introduction of farming. People had to settle down in order to erect more permanent dwellings, to plough their land and tend to their animals. Forests were cut down to create fields, around which stone walls were built. Such stone walls and organised field systems, dating back to around 4,000 years ago, have been identified on Clare Island and on the hills above Killadoon, south of Louisburgh. They have been well explored at the Céide Fields in North Mayo.

These first settlers began to build elaborate monuments for their dead, known as megalithic tombs. Along the Clew Bay Trail, there are examples of a Wedge Tomb at Srahwee (13) and a Court Tomb on Clare Island (21).

Rising Temperatures and The Bog

The end of the Stone Age came with the introduction of metal working to Ireland around 4,500 years ago. This era also saw a change in the climate.

Pl. 5 - Window of Murrisk Abbey with Croagh Patrick behind.

The climate deteriorated, with more rainfall and wind. In addition, evidence suggests that the land may have become overworked. This, coupled with the deforestation which had gone on to accommodate farming, left Ireland exposed to soil deterioration The result was the growth of blanket bog, particularly in the most vulnerable upland or exposed areas of the country, such as West Mayo.

Pl. 6 - Bog in the foreground.

However, it is this blanket bog which helped protect some of Mayo's most important evidence for human activity. The bogs provided a protective covering for the ancient field systems and stone walls, simply because they could not be touched. The field systems not covered by bog, however, were removed because of modern farming.

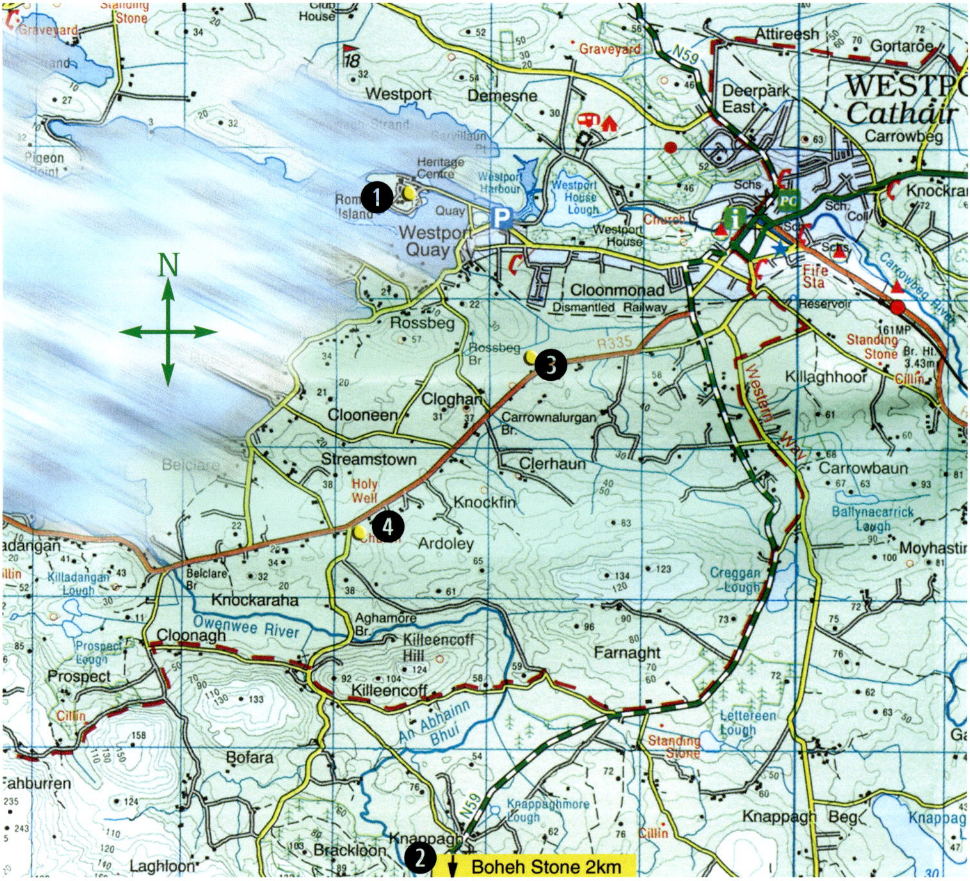

Fig. iii. - Westport Trail.
(Not to scale).

STAGE 1

Westport

cathair na mart - the stone fort of the beeves

Clew Bay

"The bay, with the Reek, which sweeps down to the sea, and a hundred islands in it, were dressed up in gold and purple, and crimson, with the whole cloudy west in a flame."

So wrote William Thackeray, who visited Clew Bay in 1842.

Clew Bay is one of Ireland's most spectacular sea inlets, stretching from Achill Island on its north side, into Westport and out to Louisburgh on its south side. It is particularly renowned for its many rounded islands, best viewed from the top of either Croagh Patrick on the bay's southern side or from the Nephin range on the bay's northern side. These islands were originally drumlins or rounded hills, gouged out of the land with the movement of ice sheets during the ice age.

An Island a Day

Popular rumour has it that there are 365 islands in the bay altogether – one for each day of the year. Few are inhabited today but some have famous owners. Dorinish More, for example, was bought by John Lennon of The Beatles. The sea angling charter boats at Westport Quay fish very close to Dorinish More so a trip to this island of retreat could be arranged. Louis Walsh, pop music mogul and manager of bands such as Westlife has bought Inis Daskey.

Bertra Beach, which lies at the north base of Croagh Patrick and faces directly west out to Clew Bay, is one of Ireland's only tombolas. A tombola is an area of sand or gravel connecting the mainland to an offshore island.

Apples Floating in the Water

It is also thought that the islands of Clew Bay could have been responsible for the ancient name given to West Mayo, Umhall (pronounced Oowel). It is not known how old this territorial name is or what it means exactly. However, since the 16th century at least, it could have been translated from the Irish word for apples, ubhall, or úll. It is thought that the islands, which resemble apples floating in water, could have given rise to this connection.

Pl. 7 - The Islands of Clew Bay.

1. Clew Bay Heritage Centre

You can start the trail from the Clew Bay Heritage Centre, which is located at the far end of the Quay in Westport, or at the Westport Tourist Office on James Street in the town centre.

Situated in a 19th century building, the Clew Bay Heritage Centre is considered a mecca for all visitors to the Westport area. It has a comprehensive museum which includes artefacts from the area, dating from the Bronze Age up to modern times, many of which relate to the sites along the Clew Bay Archaeological Trail.

Written and photographic accounts of Westport Town, Croagh Patrick and other antiquities in the surrounding region are also on display. In addition, there is a genealogical service for visitors who want to check their family roots.

SITE 2	BOHEH STONE	9.5 KM
Back to Quay Road. Right at Leenane Road junction and straight. Take left to stone after 8 km.		

Pl. 8 - Clew Bay Heritage Centre - a mecca for visitors.

2. Boheh Stone

Both Sheithe - The Skinhide Hut

Neolithic Rock Art

About eight kilometres out the Leenane Road from Westport, a large outcrop of rock at Boheh is almost totally covered in carvings or rock art. The Boheh Stone is one of two rock art sites in county Mayo and is considered one of the finest examples of neolithic rock art in Ireland and Britain.

These carvings date to the late Stone Age/Early Bronze Age, the same era in which the well-known carvings at New Grange, Dowth and Knowth in county Meath were inscribed. Many of the carvings consist of cupmarks, enclosed by one or two circles (an inspiration for the Clew Bay Archaeological Trail logo). There are also a small number of keyhole motifs.

Pl. 9 - Boheh Stone with cupmarks.

This Boheh Stone was later Christianised and called St Patrick's Chair. It is located along the pilgrimage route, Tóchar Phádraig, which runs from Ballintubber Abbey to Croagh Patrick – an example of the way in which obvious pre-Christian sites of significance were submerged into Christian rituals.

The Rolling Sun

From this outcrop there is a full view of Croagh Patrick, which led local archaeologist Gerry Bracken to explore whether there might be a relationship between the rock art and the mountain. He discovered that on two days in the year, April 18th and August 24th, the sun is seen to set on top of Croagh Patrick when viewed from the site. Then, instead of disappearing behind the mountain, the sun appears to roll down its northern shoulder. (See diagram).

Interestingly, August 24th is St Bartholomew's Day, traditionally the first day of Autumn and an important day for harvesters. It was thought that April 18th might have had similar importance as a date for sowing in prehistoric times. These two dates also split the year in three equal parts.

This suggests that these dates were used to celebrate sowing and harvesting seasons and that, indeed, there may well have been a connection between the rock art and the sacred mountain.

Cloch Bhoth Sheithe

Tá Cloch Bhoth Sheithe ar cheann de na samplaí is fearr d'ealaín chloiche neoiliteach in Éirinn agus sa Bhreatain. Tagann an snoíodóireacht – cuasghreannadh den chuid is mó, iata ag ciorcal amháin nó péire agus líon beag móitífeanna poll eochrach – ón ré chéanna ar inscríobhadh an greannadh cáiliúil ag Sí an Bhrú, Dubhadh agus Cnobha i gCo. na Mí. Tugadh íomhá Chríostaí don chloch seo níos déanaí agus tugadh Cathaoir Naomh Pádraig uirthi.

Ón lomán seo tá radharc breá ar Chruach Phádraig. Thug staraí áitiúil faoi deara go dtéann an ghrian faoi ar bharr Chruach Phádraig nuair a fhéachtar uirthi ón láthair seo an 18ú Aibreán agus an 24ú Lúnasa. Ansin, in áit di imeacht ó radharc ar chúl an tsléibhe, sleamhnaíonn an ghrian síos gualainn thuaidh an tsléibhe. Roinneann an dá dháta seo an bhliain ina trí cuid chothroma agus ceaptar go ndéantaí ceiliúradh ar shéasúir na curadóireachta agus an fhómhair ar na dátaí sin.

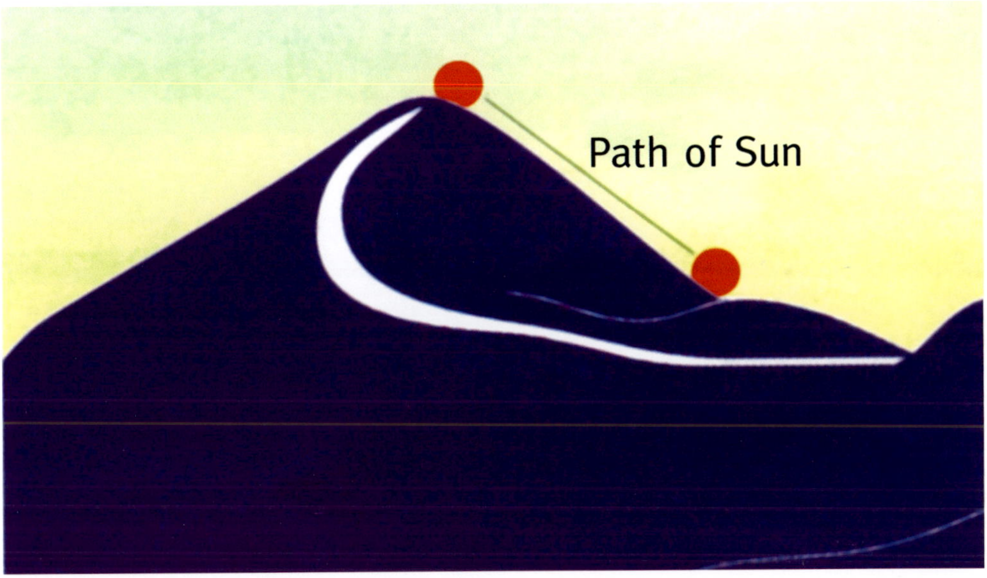

Fig. iv. - Path of the sun from Boheh on April 18th and August 24th.

SITE 3	CARROWNALURGAN RINGFORT	8.5 KM
Go back towards Westport. Take left at West Road towards Louisburgh before bridge.		

SITE 1	CLEW BAY HERITAGE CENTRE	9.5 KM
Go back towards Westport. Take left at Quay Road junction after bridge. Take right at Quay.		

3. Carrowanalurgan Ringfort

Ceathrú na Lorgan - Quarter of the Low Long Hill

Carrowanalurgan Ringfort is located on the right-hand side of the West Road from Westport to Louisburgh and is an excellent example of an early Christian settlement (500 to 1,000 AD).

Ancient Farmsteads

Ringforts were the enclosed farmsteads of their day and served as habitation sites for generations of Irish people. Usually circular in shape, their construction material depended on the geology of an area. Therefore, there are forts enclosed by an earthen bank, referred to as Raths and Lios, and others enclosed by a stone wall, referred to as Cashels, Dúns and Cahers.

The domestic house or houses only took up a small area of the fort interior. Most of the area was used for sheltering animals, either at night or for longer periods of bad weather. The entrances to these forts were generally away from the prevailing westerly winds and were located for the most part on the eastern side of the forts. Although in the case of Carrowanalurgan there is no clear trace of its original entrance.

Carrowanalurgan is classified as a univallate rath with crest-to-crest diameters of 38m north-south by 36m east-west. Like most ringforts, Carrowanalurgan is located on the highest point of a pronounced ridge with a superb view over the surrounding countryside.

Brownes of Westport

The most notable feature of the fort is a dressed limestone slab, 60 cm high, which is carved in high relief with a Latin inscription, reading:
"Orate Pro Anima Petri Browne Qui Me Fieri Fecit AD 1723." (In English) "Pray for the soul of Peter Browne for whom this was erected in AD 1723."

Carrowanalurgan was traditionally regarded as the place of worship in the penal days (when no Catholic Masses were permitted) and Peter Browne was the local patron. He was the son and successor of Colonel John Browne of Westport, a lawyer and an officer in King James's army, which was defeated in Limerick in 1691.

A further reference to Peter Browne, and also to an old church across the road from this fort, comes from A History of Mayo vol. I by Knox (page 204).

Pl. 10 - Dressed Limestone Slab.

"There was a very ancient cemetery at Carrownalurgan where stands the ruins of an old church stated to have been the parish church before the existing one was erected a little over a hundred years ago. The old church of the penal days at Carrownalurgan is stated to have been merely a barn, and near it stands an engraved stone. The inscription asks for prayers for Peter Browne, alleged to have been one of the Browne's of Westport, and the fable is told locally that this man's son, on becoming a Protestant, got the estate and kicked out the old man."

Lios Cheathrú na Lorgan

Is sampla den scoth é Lios Cheathrú na Lorgan de lonnaíocht Luath-Chríostaí (500 – 1000 AD). Bhíodh clóis feirme istigh sna Liosanna – a mbíodh cruth chiorclach de ghnáth orthu agus iad suite ar thalamh ard, mar a fheictear anseo. Ní thógadh teach cónaithe na n-áititheoirí mórán spáis agus bhí an chuid is mó den taobh istigh den Lios á úsáid chun foscadh a thabhairt d'ainmhithe.

Is í an ghné is suntasaí den lios ná leacht cóirithe aolchloiche leis an scríbhinn laidine air, a deir: "Orate Pro Anima Petri Browne Qui Me Fieri Fecit AD 1723." "Guigh d'anam Peter Browne ar tógadh seo dó in AD 1723."

Ceaptar gur dhuine de Bhrúnaigh Theach Chathair na Mart é Peter Browne. Is é an scéal atá ann gur athraigh mac an fhir seo a chreideamh, agus gur chaith sé a athair amach as an eastát.

SITE 4	OUGHAVALE (AUGHAVAL) GRAVEYARD & CHURCHES	1.5 KM
Straight ahead towards Louisburgh 1.5km. Turn left.		

SITE 2	BOHEH STONE	8.5 KM
Straight to Leenane Road junction. Turn right and straight ahead for 8 km. Take left turn.		

4. Oughavale (Aughaval) Graveyard and Churches

An Nuachongbháil - The New Foundation

This very large cemetery is the main burial ground in Westport parish today. It was originally a large and important monastery, dating to the early Christian period.

An interesting point about this graveyard is that both Catholics and Protestants used it for burials, evidenced by the variety of names on the headstones. Within the graveyard, there is a tomb to members of the Livingston family, which owned a brewery and a distillery in Westport. The family was also the town's connection to that other famous brewing family, Guinness. Mary Livingston, the widow of Richard Guinness of Dublin, is buried here at Oughavale. Another feature is the "Altóir na bPáistí" or Altar of the Children, which was erected to the memory of the children who died before being baptised. Under previous Catholic Church thinking, these children could not be given a full Christian burial.

Early Churches

There were originally churches on either side of the road. While the church on the north side of the road no longer survives, part of that on the south side is clearly visible in the graveyard.

This church at Oughavale has a square-headed doorway dating to the late 11th or early 12th century, making it one of the few examples of early church architecture in West Mayo. At the turn of the 12th century, the Romanesque style was introduced to Ireland which used round arches in the construction of doors and windows. The rest of the church building is of a later date.

This church, and the site, have strong associations with St. Colmcille. The Irish Annals record that Ó Máille was murdered in this stone church in 1131 AD by the son of Donal O'Dowda, but the murderer was himself killed by his own spear within three months *"through the miracle of Columcille."*

Pl. 11 - Square headed doorway dates to 11th or early 12th Century.

Cursing Stone

John O'Donovan, who visited the site in 1838, was told of a magic stone called Leac Cholumb Cille, which people turned to wish each other bad luck. However, the stone was broken by order of the priest in the 18th century.

St Patrick's Knee

The graveyard to the north of the road has more of an association with St Patrick. In this part of the graveyard is a stone with a large but shallow hollow, where the saint was supposed to have prayed, giving rise to the name Gloonpatrick, *glúin Phádraig,* or Patrick's knee. Gloonpatrick lies directly to the left of the stile into this graveyard off the West Road. Tradition upholds that the stone never goes dry.

Pl. 12 - Gloonpatrick never goes dry.

These type of stones are known as Bullaun Stones by archaeologists and are common finds on monastic sites. They were more probably associated with metalworking.

There is also an inscribed Quern stone from this site, originally used for grinding corn, on view at the Westport Heritage Centre.

Reilig agus Séipéil Oughavale - An Nuachongbháil

Is í Oughavale an phríomhreilig i bparóiste Chathair na Mart inniu agus tá sí sách neamhghnách mar go bhfuil idir Chaitlicigh agus Phrotastúnaigh curtha inti. Ba láthair mhór agus thábhachtach mainistreach luath-Chríostaí a bhí anseo tráth agus bhíodh séipéil ar gach aon taobh den bhóthar. Níl ach fothrach amháin ar marthain fós áfach. Tá a doras le ceann cearnógach ar cheann de na corrshamplaí d'ailtireacht luathchríostaí in Iarthar Mhaigh Eo. De réir an tseanchais bhíodh cloch dhraíochta ar an láthair seo ar a dtugtaí Leac Cholm Cille a bhíodh á húsáid ag daoine chun mí-ádh a ghuí ar a chéile. Briseadh an chloch ar ordú sagairt san 18ú haois.

Bhí baint ag an reilig ó thuaidh den bhóthar le Naomh Pádraig. Tá cloch anseo a bhfuil dhá chuas inti, áit a ndeirtear a mbíodh an naomh ag guí, agus is as sin a thagann an t-ainm Glúin Phádraig. Tugtar Balláin ar na clocha seo sa seandálaíocht agus is dóichí go raibh baint acu le miotalóireacht.

SITE 5	ANNAGH - KILLADANGAN ARCHAEOLOGICAL COMPLEX	3 KM
From graveyard gates, left at West Road. Straight at junction with Coast Road for 2 km.		

SITE 3	CARROWNALURGAN RINGFORT	1.5 KM
From graveyard gates, right at West Road. Straight.		

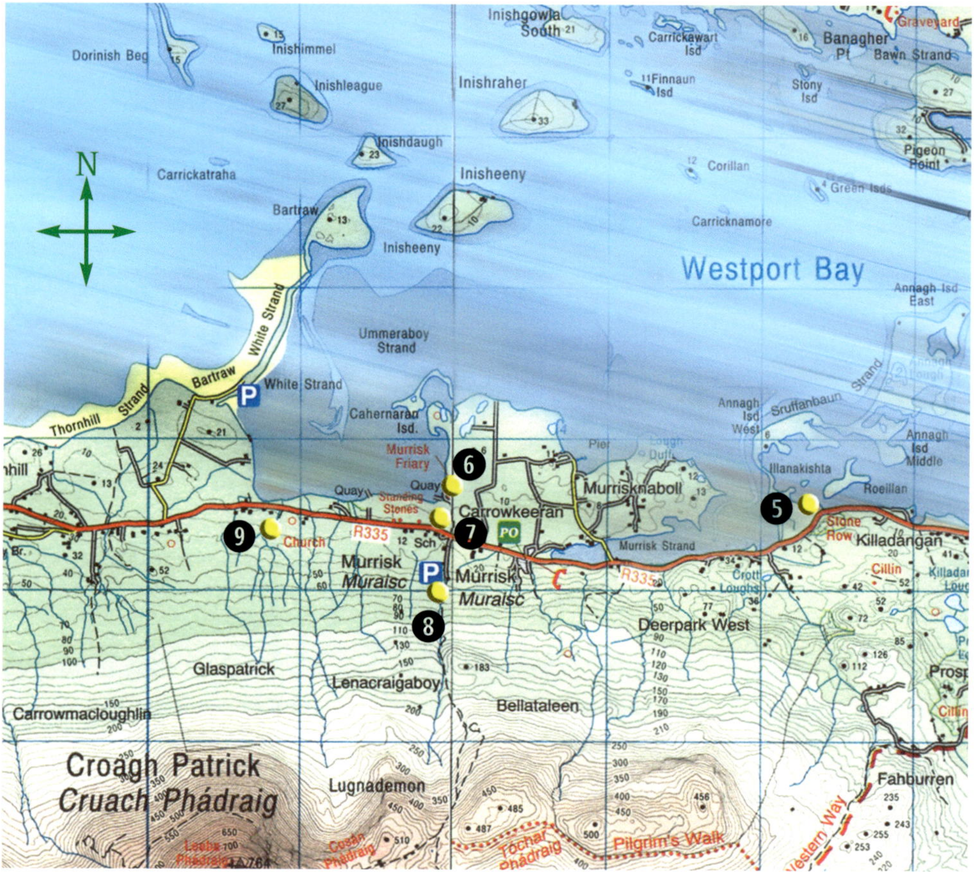

Fig. v. - Murrisk Trail.
(Not to scale).

STAGE 11

Murrisk

muraisc - sea marsh

Croagh Patrick

"To admire the Reek is to pray"

Croagh Patrick, or The Reek, as it is commonly known, is not on the Clew Bay Archaeological Trail. However, it cannot be ignored in a guidebook about West Mayo. It dominates the skyline, rising to a height of 765 metres. It was originally called Cruachán Aigli. Cruach means conical mountain or stacked-up hill. Murrisk, at its base was called Muiresc Aigli, indicating that the overall area was called Aigli, which means eagle.

Pl. 14 - The mountain in Summer.

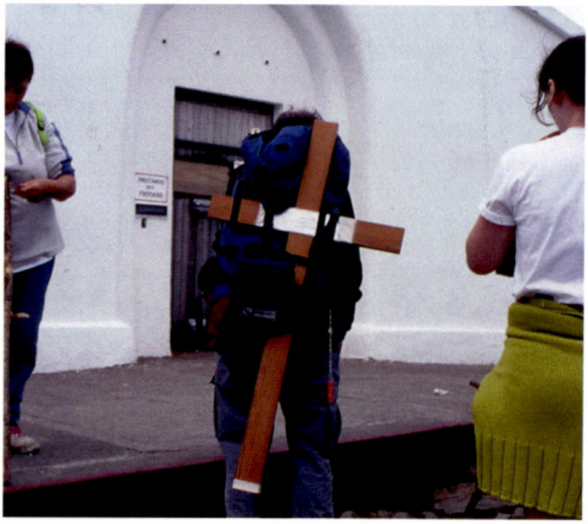

Pl. 13 - A pilgrim carrying a cross arrives on the summit.

Ireland's Holy Mountain

It is not just its physical presence that distinguishes Croagh Patrick. It is Ireland's Holy Mountain where, according to tradition and early accounts, St Patrick fasted for forty days and nights on its summit, following the example of Christ and Moses.

Others have also spent long periods of time on the reek. In the early 19th century, Robert Binn, commonly known as "Bob of the Reek" lived on the summit for 14 years, doing penance for those who couldn't visit the mountain themselves.

Pilgrimage

Since St Patrick's visit, the mountain has been a focus for Christian worship and pilgrimage. In the Ulster Annals it is recorded that a thunderstorm resulted in the death of 30 pilgrims to the mountain on the evening of St Patrick's Day in 1113 AD.

Today, over 100,000 people still climb the mountain every year, many of them on the last Sunday of July or "Reek Sunday," and some of them in their bare feet. The pilgrims perform penitential exercises, known as the Stations of the Reek, either walking around or kneeling at stone cairns and repeating specified prayers. This annual pilgrimage used to take place at night – a tradition which ended in 1973. Services are also available on the mountain on the last Friday of July or "Garland Friday," when traditionally locals climb the mountain, and on August 15th, the Feast of the Assumption.

Pl. 15 - Pilgrim's Rest.

Pagan Roots

Like many Christian traditions and locations, the root for Croagh Patrick's "holiness" can be traced to Pagan traditions. For example, the festival of Lughnasa was the start of the harvest festival in honour of the God Lugh, who was an ancient pagan god of the Tuatha Dé Danann, a divine race. This harvest festival was absorbed into new Christian beliefs and, locally, the festival became known as Domhnach na Cruaiche or Reek Sunday, the most popular day for pilgrimage.

Summit Civilisation

Long before the arrival of Christianity, a hill fort, complete with stone ramparts and dwellings occupied the summit. Some amber, blue and black glass beads dating to the 3rd century BC were found near the collapsed wall of this rampart during archaeological excavations by Mayo County Archaeologist Gerry Walsh. In addition, the outline of at least 30 hut sites have been discovered on the mountain slopes outside of the rampart

Fig. vi - Computer generated image of the original hill fort showing the entrance on the east side of the summit.

Churches and Relics

Excavations on the summit have uncovered the foundations of an early Christian oratory, carbon dating from 430 to 890 AD. The present church was built on the summit in 1905. It took 12 local men six months to build the oratory, which was constructed using local stone and cement, brought up the mountain by donkey and horseback.

The Black Bell of St Patrick was a highly venerated relic on Croagh Patrick for many years. Tradition has it that the Bell was originally of white metal, but became black because it was used as a weapon against the demons which came to torment St Patrick on the Reek. The Bell dates from 600 to 900 AD and is now in the possession of the National Museum of Ireland.

Pl. 16 - Oratory with Clew Bay.

Banishing the Snakes

Legend has it that Ireland was pestered with a triple plague, namely, *"a great abundance of venomous reptiles, with myriads of demons visibly appearing, and with multitude of magicians"* (P.L. O'Madden – Cruach Phádraig – 1929).

But, St Patrick *"laboured by prayer and other exercises of devotion to deliver the island from the triple pestilence. Taking the Staff of Jesus into his hand he hurled the reptiles into Log na nDeamhan."* Log na nDeamhan, or the demon's hollow, is a lake at the north base of Croagh Patrick, which, it is said, burst up because of the force with which St Patrick hurled the same reptiles.

Famous Visitors

One of the most famous visitors was Princess and film star, Grace Kelly, who visited the mountain with her husband Prince Rainier of Monaco on June 21, 1961. Grace Kelly's grandfather came from Drimurla, Newport, on the north side of Clew Bay.

5. Annagh-Killadangan Archaeological Complex

Eanach - Marsh
Choill an Daingin - The Wood of the Fortress

Bronze Age Collection

This collection of ancient monuments lies in an area currently occupied by a salt marsh on the south eastern shore of Clew Bay. In earlier millennia the high tides would not have troubled these sites. However, today, while the site is accessible for the majority of the year, it can be submerged during Spring tides.

The collection of monuments, probably dating from the Bronze Age, includes an oval shaped enclosure, with a fine stone row, as well as a possible stone circle, and a possible fulacht fiadh (bronze-age cooking area). This grouping of monuments suggests that this was a major ceremonial site.

Pl. 17 - Stone alignment.

Standing Stones

The oval enclosure is visible on the edge of the high water tidemark (see aerial view on the next page). However, what is most remarkable about the enclosure is the row of five standing stones; four stones are upright and the fifth has fallen down. The fifth fallen stone has an angular or pointed shape, which would have pointed towards the Reek.

The function of such stone alignments remains largely a mystery. Some examples have been found to mark bronze age burials. Others are thought to be territorial markers or markers for recording places where important events took place. Others seem to mark key solar and lunar events.

Winter Solstice Alignment

This is thought to be the most likely reason for the standing stones at Killadangan. This stone alignment increases in height from north to south, drawing the eye up to a niche in the eastern shoulder of Croagh Patrick. On December 21st, the winter solstice, at about 1:50 pm, the sun dips into this little niche or kink in the mountain. At this point, the sun is directly in line with the row of stones, before disappearing shortly afterwards behind the mountain.

Pl. 18 - Annagh in Winter.

Lazy Servant

A folk tale associated with these stones was recalled at the turn of the 19th century by James Berry, a local storyteller. The King of Killadangan was the brother of the first husband of Queen Maeve, the powerful Celtic Queen of the west of Ireland. While the name of the king has disappeared, the name of his lazy servant, Thulera, has remained in folk memory. The king attempted to force the sea and tide under his command. But as he waited for the incoming tide, the servant fell asleep, leaving the king to fight the waves on his own. Both the king and the lazy servant drowned.

Coimpléasc Seandálaíochta Eanach – Choill an Daingin

Agus tú ag féachaint ar an mbailiúchán seo de shéadchomharthaí ársa bíonn tú i do sheasamh ar riasc goirt, a bhíonn faoi uisce go minic nuair a bhíonn sé ina lánmhara. Na mílte bliain ó shin, áfach, ní bhíodh an lánmhara ag cur isteach ar na láithreacha seo.

I measc an bhailiúcháin séadchomharthaí, ón gCré-Umhaois is dócha, tá iatán ubhchruthach, alíniú liag, galláin agus b'fhéidir fulacht fia (áit a mbítí ag cócaireacht sa Chré-Umhaois).

Is é an rud is suntasaí faoin iatán ná an t-ailíniú liag (ceithre ghallán, a bhfuil ceann díobh tite) agus ardaíonn ón gceann ó thuaidh go dtí an ceann ó dheas, rud a tharraingíonn an tsúil ar chuas i ngualainn thoir Chruach Phádraig. Ar an 21ú Nollaig, grianstad an gheimhridh, ag thart ar 1.50 p.m., íslíonn an ghrian isteach sa chuas nó sa scoilt bheag seo sa sliabh. Ag an tráth sin, bíonn an ghrian díreach in aon líne leis an tsraith liag, sula n-imíonn sí ó radharc ar chúl an tsléibhe go gairid ina dhiaidh sin.

Pl. 19 - Aerial view of Annagh-Killadangan complex.

SITE 6,7,8	MURRISK ABBEY NATIONAL FAMINE MONUMENT ST. PATRICK'S STATUE	2.5 KM	
Straight ahead towards Louisburgh.			

SITE 4	OUGHAVALE (AUGHAVAL) GRAVEYARD & CHURCHES	3 KM	
Straight towards Westport to junction of Coast Road with West Road. Right onto West Road and first right.			

6. Murrisk Abbey

The small Augustinian Friary of Murrisk is a well-known ancient landmark which lies at the sea shore at the north base of Croagh Patrick.

It was a chief of the O'Malleys, Thady O'Malley, who donated land in 1457 for a friary and church. The Augustinians set up the Friary because *"the inhabitants of those parts have not hitherto been instructed in their faith."*

Soon after its foundation, it became more popular to begin pilgrimages to Croagh Patrick at Murrisk – a tradition that continues today. Up to then, the pilgrimage started from Aughagower and continued to Croagh Patrick along the Tóchar Phádraig, which approaches the mountain from its southeastern side.

A Persecuted Community

In 1578, the lands belonging to the Abbey were leased to James Garvey, brother of John Garvey, the Church of Ireland Archbishop of Armagh. While very little is known about the circumstances of the friars between then and the 1700s, when the Abbey finally ceased to function, it is known that the community most likely suffered persecution. One friar, Fr. Myles Prendergast, OSA, spent many years on the run in the area of Clifden. Others are thought to have lived in the area around Murrisk often administering to their flock outdoors. The last monk based in Murrisk appears to be a Fr. Philip Staunton, who left in the 1870s. One of the last celebrations of mass at the Abbey was in 1942 by Fr. James Campbell, a relative of the Campbells who run the well-known pub at the base of the Reek.

Pl. 20 - Murrisk Abbey - founded in 1457.

Augustinian Church

The ruins consist of an L-shaped building representing the church, the sacristy and the chapter room with overhead dormitory. The church is long and narrow, a shape typical of Augustinian churches. There is a beautiful east window with carved human heads on the wall outside. The south wall is crowned with unusual battlements and a number of trefoil and ogee headed windows. There was a belfry tower at the west end of the church, inserted after the church itself was completed. However, the church outlived its new addition; all that survives of this tower now is a ribbed vault.

The east end of the church gives access to the sacristy and stone stairs leading to the dormitory on the first floor (through a small door in the north wall of the east end, beside a holy water fountain). North of the sacristy is the chapter room, where friars met to discuss the day's issues and to read. There are no traces of the domestic buildings which would have accompanied the Abbey, such as the refectory, kitchen or cellars.

Pl. 21 - Main window.

Mainistir Mhuraisce

Deirtear gur bhunaigh na Manaigh Agaistíneacha Mainistir Mhuraisce in 1456 mar gheall nach raibh teagasc faighte ag na daoine a chónaigh sa cheantar sin ar an gcreideamh. Ba ghearr go mba é an pointe tosaigh é d'oilithreachtaí suas Cruach Phádraig. Roimhe sin, thugadh oilithrigh faoin sliabh ó Thóchar Phádraig, ag tosú in Áth an Ghabhair.

Is foirgneamh i gcruth L atá san fhoirgneamh a léiríonn séipéal fada cúng, an sacraistí agus an seomra caibidle le suanlios os a chionn. Tá fuinneog álainn ar an taobh thoir agus tá cinn daoine snoite ar an mballa lasmuigh. Tá táibhle ar an mballa ó dheas agus fuinneoga trédhuilleacha agus ceannchíoma. Bhíodh cloigtheach ag ceann thiar an tséipéil, a cuireadh isteach tar éis an séipéal féin a bheith críochnaithe. Mar sin féin, is faide a mhair an séipéal ná an píosa nua a cuireadh leis; ní mhaireann den tur anois ach boghta iomaireach.

Pl. 22 - Window detail on the south wall.

7. National Famine Monument

Mayo was hard hit by the Great Famine of the mid-1840s when the potato crop, the staple diet for Irish small farmers and landless day labourers, failed for four years in succession. There were many reports of evictions, heartless landlords and starving tenants. By the time the famine had ended, one million of the weakest had died and millions had left the land. The Irish Famine resulted in the single greatest loss of life in 19th century Europe and had a devastating impact on the Irish language and culture.

Pl. 23 - Sails like skeletons.

Coffin Ships

Merchants bringing food supplies to Ireland from abroad at this time used human cargo to make money out of their return sailings. Instead of returning to their own ports with empty hulls, they filled their ships with wretched people trying to escape starvation. Needless to say, these ships were rarely equipped to take passengers. There was overcrowding and poor sanitation. But they were cheap passages, and generally the only affordable form of transport to the United States, Britain, and Australia for the poor Irish.

But, many did not even get to these destinations. Tens of thousands crowded into the industrial cities of Britain unable to afford the passage further. For those who could afford the onward passage, their outcome was often no better; thousands died during the crossings, lending the name coffin ships to these ill-fated vessels.

Sails like Skeletons

The National Famine Monument was unveiled in July 1997 by President Mary Robinson. Created by renowned sculptor, John Behan, the monument is cast in bronze and depicts a coffin ship. However, the sails on this famine ship are fashioned like skeletons, representing the misery of the trip to the New World for millions.

Sister Monument

In 2001, a sister monument was unveiled outside the United Nations building in New York. The New York ship has two gangplanks with survivors emerging onto land after their trip across the Atlantic Ocean.

Séadchomhartha Náisiúnta an Ghorta

Nocht an tUachtarán Máire Mhic Róibín Séadchomhartha Náisiúnta an Ghorta i mí Iúil 1997. Ba é John Behan a dhear é agus teilgeadh an séadchomhartha i gcré-umha agus léiríonn sé a raibh ar eolas faoi na longa báis. Tá seolta an loing múnlaithe mar chreatlaigh, rud a léiríonn an ainnise a bhain leis an aistear chuig an Domhan Nua do na milliúin duine.

In 2001, nochtadh comh-shéadchomhartha lasmuigh d'fhoirgneamh na Náisiún Aontaithe i Nua Eabhrac. Tá dhá stangairt ar long Nua Eabhrac, áfach, a léiríonn na daoine a mhair tríd an anó ag teacht i dtír tar éis an aistir trasna na Farraige Móire.

8. Statue of St Patrick

The Statue of St Patrick at the start of the traditional pilgrim route up Croagh Patrick was erected in 1928 by Fr. Patrick Patterson. The statue was erected with money collected in America for rebuilding St Mary's Church in Westport. A press report in The Mayo News, on June 30th, 1928 stated:

"The new shrine is placed at an early stage of the pilgrim's way, and in such a position that even the most feeble can reach this spot without any difficulty. We foresee that it will be a source of great devotion. It will, so to speak, hearten and give courage to those who are entering the rigours of the ascent, while it will service as a thanks-giving shrine to those who are returning wearied from the penitential exercises. It will no doubt be a great place of rendezvous for pilgrims both ascending and descending. From it many a prayer both of petition and thanks-giving will ascend to St. Patrick in Heaven."

While the statue is not one of the traditional stations along the pilgrim route, it is used by most people as a starting and finishing point for their journey up the mountain.

Dealbh de Naomh Pádraig

Tá an Dealbh de Naomh Pádraig ag tús an bhealaigh oilithreachta traidisiúnta suas Cruach Phádraig agus is é an tAthair Patrick Patterson a thóg í sa bhliain 1928.

Cé nach ceann de na stáisiúin thraidisiúnta í an dealbh ar an mbealach oilithreachta, baineann formhór na ndaoine úsáid aisti mar an pointe tosaigh agus an pointe deiridh den aistear suas an sliabh.

Pl. 24 - Statue of St. Patrick, "A source of great devotion".

SITE 9	GLASPATRICK CHURCH	1 KM
Straight ahead towards Louisburgh.		

SITE 5	KILLADANGAN - ANNAGH ARCHAEOLOGICAL COMPLEX	2.5 KM
Straight ahead towards Westport.		

9. Glaspatrick Church
Glaise Phádraig - Patrick's Stream

The townland of Glaspatrick runs all the way from the top of Croagh Patrick to the sea level below this site. The remains of the church and graveyard take their name from this stream.

Pl. 25 - Large stones used in construction.

The remains are largely overgrown with briars, and while the west gable of the church is gone and the east gable has been reduced to the foundations, the proportions of the church suggest that it belongs to the early medieval period – probably early 12th century. This is further evidenced by the large stones used in its construction.

Glaspatrick was one of the original churches founded by St Patrick in the area, along with Aughagower and Teampall Padraig on the summit of Croagh Patrick. The See of Armagh, as successors to St Patrick, claimed these three churches. However, the See of Tuam also claimed the churches. This argument continued until the 13th century when the Papacy upheld the claim of Tuam to these sites, as they had maintained the early Patrician churches.

Another of Glaspatrick's connections to St Patrick is through a man named Totmáel, who was the saint's charioteer. Totmáel is said to have died in the area and to have been buried in Glaspatrick. A large pillar with markings on it stood in the graveyard until the middle of this century and most likely marked an important grave, possibly that of Totmáel's.

While the burial ground at Glaspatrick is ancient, most of the inscriptions are fairly modern, and it is still used for occasional burials. Glaspatrick was used as a graveyard for the islanders – those who lived on the small islands within Clew Bay.

Old Head

On your way to the next site, you will see a prominent rounded and wooded headland in front of you. This is called Old Head and its covering is the only oak forest on the Western sea board.

Glaise Phádraig

Tá fásra de dhriseacha scaipthe cuid mhór ar fhothrach an tséipéil seo. Mar sin féin, cé go bhfuil an bhinn thiar den séipéal imithe agus go bhfuil an bhinn thoir tite go dtí an bhunshraith, tugann buntomhais an tséipéil le tuiscint go mbaineann sé le tréimhe sa luathmheánaois – is dócha go luath sa 12ú haois. Tá tuilleadh fianaise air sin sna clocha móra a úsáideadh ina thógáil.

Faigheann an séipéal agus an ceantar máguaird a ainm ó shruthán in aice láimhe, Glaise Phádraig, Sruthán Phádraig. Mar sin féin, is é an ceangal is cáiliúla atá aige le Naomh Pádraig ná an fear darbh ainm Totmaol, carbadóir an naoimh, a deirtear a cailleadh sa cheantar agus a cuireadh ar an láthair seo.

Pl. 26 - Small size suggests Glaspatrick church was built in the early medieval period.

SITE 10	KILGEEVER ABBEY	10 KM	
Straight towards Louisburgh for 8km. Turn left. Left again and take first right.			

SITE 6,7,8	MURRISK ABBEY NATIONAL FAMINE MONUMENT ST. PATRICK'S STATUE	1 KM	
Straight towards Westport.			

Fig. vii. - Louisburgh Trail.
(Not to scale).

STAGE III

Louisburgh

Cluain Cearbhán - the meadow of the buttercups

10. Kilgeever Abbey
Cill Ghaobhair – The Near Church

Kilgeever Abbey was traditionally where pilgrims stopped to perform stations on the turas, or journey, from Croagh Patrick to Caher Island. Little is known about the history of this site, even though it appears to have been the parish church throughout the late medieval period.

The Abbey is rectangular with a 12th century round-headed window in the eastern gable. Towards the eastern end of the church are two aumbries (small cupboards or niches used for storing vessels) in the walls. Towards the western end of the south wall is a 15th century door with a pock-dressed (roughly faced and

Pl. 27 - Pock markings on doorway.

shaped stone) arch and a draw-bar hole to secure a beam that locked the door. The west gable is now reduced to a grass-covered foundation. However, when the site was visited and recorded in 1838 it was still standing, and was described and sketched as a block-up flat-lintelled doorway, "5 feet 4 inches high and 2 feet 4 inches broad."

Cross Slabs

In the graveyard are two cross slabs, dating from the 7th century AD. One is a small pillar standing east-southeast of the church, featuring a cross with dovetail terminals. A second slab has a similar cross incised on it.

Pl. 28 - Cross inscribed pillar.

Holy Well

Beside the entrance to the present graveyard is a spring well, above which is a modern stone monument. The well is known locally as the "*Tobar Rí an Dhomhnaigh*", meaning "Our Lord's well of the Sabbath", where pilgrims came in large numbers on July 15th, the Festival of the 12 Apostles. Many still visit the well as part of their pilgrimage to Croagh Patrick on Reek Sunday (last Sunday of July).

The traditional stations for pilgrimage are outlined on a plaque at the gate of the graveyard and here below. You can also see where pilgrims have inscribed crosses on the rocks around which the stations are performed. This could be seen as the creation of the archaeology of the future.

Pl. 29 - Pilgrim inscriptions, archaeology of the future.

Station at Kilgeever

The traditional station begins with a circle about the blessed well while the pilgrim forms his intention. Then, kneeling opposite the well, he says seven Paters, seven Aves and the Creed. He then circles the well seven times praying and kneels again to repeat seven Paters, seven Aves and the Creed. He now walks to the three flagstones south of the well, where he says five Paters, Aves and the Creed kneeling.
At St. Patrick's Rock he kneels and says three Paters, Aves and the Creed, and entering the Abbey from the east, he says seven Paters, Aves and the Creed for the dead.

He walks back by the stream towards the blessed well where he contemplates the station by circling three times in honour of the blessed Trinity.

Custom has embellished these exercises. It is customary to count the rounds of the well by picking seven stones and dropping one at each round. Returning to the well it is usual to walk in the water if the station is for a living person. Before leaving, the pilgrim prays for Henry Murphy of Castlebar, who had the cross erected over the well.

Deserted Village

Some 400 metres to the northeast of the Holy Well is a cluster of ruined houses. This is a typical example of a deserted village. In Kilgeever, the population fell from 2,200 families in 1846 to just 600 families in 1900.

Mainistir Chill Ghaobhair

Is ag Mainistir Chill Ghaobhair a stopadh na hoilithrigh chun stáisiúin a dhéanamh ar an turas ó Chruach Phádraig go hOileán na Cathrach. Tá an stáisiún scríofa ag an ngeata.

Tá fuinneog cruinnchinn ón dara haois déag i mbinn thoir an tséipéil dhronuilligh. Ag ceann thoir an tséipéil tá dhá almóir (cófraí beaga nó cuasa chun soithí a stóráil) sna ballaí. Ag an gceann thiar agus ar an mballa ó dheas tá doras ón gcúigiú haois déag ar a bhfuil áirse póc-chóirithe (cloch gharbhéadain mhúnlaithe).

Sa reilig tá dhá chrosleacht, dar dáta an seachtú haois AD, ar a bhfuil gearrthacha ar chruth V. Tugtar Tobar Rí an Dhomhnaigh ar an bhfuarán atá ina aice an bhealaigh isteach chuig an reilig atá ann faoi láthair, áit a dtagadh oilithrigh ina sluaite ar an 15ú Iúil, Féile an dá Aspal déag.

SITE 11	LIME KILN, MONEEN	1 KM
Turn around. Left at first junction. Take second right.		

SITE 9	GLASPATRICK CHURCH	10 KM
Turn around. Left at first junction. Take first right and right again at Louisburgh Road.		

11. Lime Kiln, Moneen
Móinín - Small Bog

Fertilising and Whitewash

There was a time not so long ago when most farms in rural Ireland had their own lime kilns.

Kilns consisted of a bowl and a flue. Crushed limestone was placed in the bowl and burnt, producing lime for use as fertiliser in the fields and also for whitewashing cottages. Most of the lime kilns around the country have been destroyed and only rare examples survive. This site survives in its entirety and is as fine an example of its type to be found in the area.

Lime kilns date from the 18th Century and were in use until the 1940s in some areas.

Tornóg Aoil – Móinín

Tosaíodh ag baint úsáide as tornóga aoil san 18ú haois agus bhí siad fós á n-úsáid i roinnt áiteanna go dtí na 1940idí. Trí thine a lasadh sna tornóga seo agus cloch aoil bhrúite a chur síos ann, rinneadh aol do leasú sna garraithe agus freisin chun aol a chur ar bhallaí na dtithe. Tá formhór na dtornóg ar fud na tíre scriosta anois agus is fíorbheag eiseamlár díobh atá ar marthain. Maireann an láthair seo ina hiomláine agus is sampla den scoth é dá chineál atá le fáil sa cheantar.

Pl. 30 - Lime kilns were a feature of most farms.

SITE 12	FAMINE MUSEUM AND GRÁINNE UAILE CENTRE, LOUISBURGH	2 KM	
Turn around, right at junction and straight through cross roads in Louisburgh.			

SITE 10	KILGEEVER ABBEY	1 KM	
Turn around. Left at junction. Take first right.			

12. Famine Museum & Granuaile Centre, Louisburgh

Famine Memories

The famine has afflicted all parts of Ireland to some degree, but because of the horrific happenings in Mayo its cruel memory is particularly poignant.

This abstract from an article by James Browne, Parish Priest of Ballintubber and Burriscarra, from the *Mayo Constitution*, 1849, gives some indication of the double desperation of starvation and eviction at the time.

"I find that at least eight hundred houses have been levelled to the ground, that three thousand human beings have been swept away by famine and disease and that 500 have fled to America or England....
The small farmers who have pawned the clothes off their backs to make a tillage have not a morsel to eat – there is neither public nor private employment in these two parishes, and unless the Almighty, in his mercy, inspire the hearts of the friends of the poor to come to our rescue, the lives of 4000 human beings are this moment doomed to suffer all the horrors of death by starvation."

All along the Clew Bay Archaeological Trail, there are the remains of the famine landscape – raised rows of potato drills, often dug out of the most inhospitable and barren of land.

Local Memories

The Famine Museum in Louisburgh recounts local memories of the famine, presents coverage of the famine in the media, nationally and locally, and shows how links have been established between Louisburgh and other parts of the world, culminating in the local famine walk along the Doo Lough Valley.

Granuaile – O'Malley Chief

The Granuaile Centre recounts the life and times of the 16th century O'Malley Chief and Sea Captain, Granuaile (Grace O'Malley or Gráinne Uaile) who headed the shipping fleet which reigned supreme in Clew Bay at that time.

The Centre opens seasonally.
Telephone: 098-66341.

Pl. 31 - Louisburgh Centre.

Músaem an Ghorta agus Ionad Ghráinne Mhaoil, Cluain Cearbhán

Déanann Músaem an Ghorta i gCluain Cearbhán cur síos ar na cuimhní áitiúla atá ar an nGorta Mór, cuirtear an trácht a bhí ar an nGorta sna meáin, go náisiúnta agus go háitiúil, i láthair agus taipeántar mar a bunaíodh naisc idir Cluain Cearbhán agus codanna eile den domhan, agus tá siúlóid ar feadh Ghleann Dhúloch mar chríoch air.

Tugann Ionad Ghráinne Uaile cuntas ar an saol mar a bhí sa 16ú haois le linn ré an Taoisigh agus an Chaptaen Loinge Gráinne Uaile (nó Gráinne Ní Mháille) a bhí i gceann feadhna ar chabhlach long a raibh ceannas ceann acu i gCuan Mó ag an am.

Pl. 32 - Granuaile Centre.

SITE 13	SRAHWEE OR ALTÓIR WEDGE TOMB	9.5 KM	
Right at cross roads. First left after bridge. Straight for 8 km to second right. Over river and right.			

SITE 11	LIME KILN, MONEEN	2 KM	
Straight at cross roads. Left.			

13. Srahwee or Altóir Megalithic Wedge Tomb

Sraith Bhuí - The Yellow River Land

One of the finest megalithic tombs in Ireland is located at Srahwee. This particular example is a wedge tomb.

They are so called because of their wedge shape; wider and higher at the entrance and gradually tapering towards the rear. This type of tomb generally dates to the beginning of the Bronze Age (about 2,500 BC), when there was a final flourish of tomb building in Ireland.

The gallery is 4.2m long and is closed on the east end by a single back stone. A septal stone 1.4m long and 1m high divides the main chamber, leaving a gap of 0.3m. The portico is currently defined by two stones on the south and one stone on the north and is open to the west-northwest. A second stone on the north has fallen into the portico.

Penal Altar

The flat roof stone was used as an altar during Penal times in the early 18th century, giving the tomb its local name, *Altóir*, meaning altar. It has a primitive incised cross at the upper surface at the southeastern end. Locals also call the site The Holy Well.

Ancient Forest

One hundred metres southwest of the tomb is one of the best examples of an ancient forest to be seen in the country. The stumps of 4,500 year-old trees are visible in the cutaway bog in and around the lake.

Sraith Bhuí nó Altóir

Seo ceann de na tuamaí meigiliteacha is fearr in Éirinn. Is sampla de thuama dingeach é an ceann áirithe seo, a ainmnítear mar gheall ar a chruth, é níos leithne agus níos airde ag an mbealach isteach agus ag caolú isteach i dtreo a dheiridh. Tógadh an cineál seo tuama ag tús na Cré-Umhaoise (thart ar 2000 BC), nuair a bhí an borradh deiridh faoi thógáil tuamaí in Éirinn.

Baineadh úsáid as an díon cothrom cloiche mar altóir le linn na bPéindlithe, agus is as sin a thagann an t-ainm áitiúil, Altóir. Tá cros bhunaidh gearrtha isteach ar an dromchla uachtarach ag an gceann thoir-theas de.

Má bhreathnaítear 100 méadar siar ó dheas ón tuama, tá ceann de na samplaí is fearr in Éirinn d'fhoraois ársa le feiceáil sa lagphortach agus sa loch.

Pl. 33 - Srahwee - one the finest megalithic tombs in Ireland.

SITE 14	BUNLAHINCH CLAPPERBRIDGE	5 KM
Straight ahead to cross roads. Through cross roads and take last right.		

SITE 12	FAMINE MUSEUM AND GRÁINNE UAILE CENTRE, LOUISBURGH	9.5 KM
Straight and over bridge. Take left at Leenane Road junction. Straight for 8 km. Right at Louisburgh and right again at Louisburgh cross roads.		

14. Bunlahinch Clapperbridge
Bún na hInse -
Bottom of the river meadow

Situated about seven kilometres southwest of Louisburgh, on the Bunleemshough River, is a Clapperbridge, a very unusual feature in the west of Ireland. The word clapper originally meant plank in the Sussex area of England, where there are many examples of these bridges

Foot bridge

The basic structure of a Clapperbridge consists of small stone piers or pillars, which are spanned by flat stone slabs or planks. It is a footbridge designed to cross wide, flat streams and rivers. The water can rise up easily over it, washing away through the holes between the stone piers without doing any damage to the bridge.

It is a prehistoric form of stone bridge. In the UK, many Clapperbridges date from Roman times. However, most were built at a later time.

The Colony and Jumpers

It is likely that this bridge was built in the 1840s or 50s. The Ordnance Survey map from 1837 indicates stepping stones only where the bridge now exists.

It is also likely that the bridge was built as part of work carried out by the Irish Church Mission, a Protestant community or colony, led by Hugh Gordon, known as a "jumper" or a person who changed his religion. The word jumper comes from the Irish *D'iompaigh,* pronounced Jumpee, meaning to change over. Considering the time, there was debate over whether Catholics "jumped" for religious reasons or for "the yellow corn", given out during the Great Famine.

The Marquis of Sligo, who evicted the original villagers, gave the land to the Mission rent-free. It was reported in 1850 that the
"General Irish Reformation Society, which has built a church at Bunlahinch is about to build a school house and pays the master and mistress: also pays a scripture reader."

Pl. 34 - Clapperbridge - thought to have been built as part of a religious mission.

It was also said that the Mission's church was opened in the presence of 300, all of whom prayed through Irish – a report hotly contested by Fr. Myles Sheridan, P.P., who wrote;

"I have seen in the last Constitution a most false and pompous display of an exhibition at Bunlehinch on Sunday last, where, it is stated, a congregation of 300 persons attended. Now, in this parish, there was not twelve of those persons called Jumpers, and these are, in other words, wretched paupers, who could get no relief from the Parson unless they appeared at Church on Sunday – Monday being the day of distribution of the charity meal."

Locally, the area is still referred to as The Colony.

Droichead Lindéir Bhun Leath Inse [Bun na hInse]

Is gné neamhghnách amach is amach é an droichead lindéir seo in Iarthar na hÉireann. Is sail an bhunbhrí a bhí leis an bhfocal lindéar i gceantar Sussex i Sasana, áit a bhfuil samplaí go leor de le fáil. Is cineál droichid cloiche réamhstairiúil é an droichead lindéir. Tá an struchtúr bunúsach déanta as piaraí nó piléir bheaga cloiche, a bhíonn trasnaithe ag leachtanna cothroma cloiche nó ag saileanna. Dearadh iad chun aibhneacha agus srutháin leathana, cothroma a thrasnú, mar a fheictear anseo, agus baineadh úsáid astu mar dhroichid coise.

Is é is dóichí gur tógadh an droichead seo sna 1840idí nó 1850idí mar chuid den obair a rinne Misean Eaglais na hÉireann, pobal nó coilíneacht Phrotastúnach ar thug Marcas Shligigh talamh saor ó chíos dóibh. Tugtar an Choilíneacht go háitiúil ar an gceantar go fóill.

SITE 15	KILLEEN GRAVEYARD AND CROSS SLAB	1 KM	
Back to Killeen cross roads and left.			

SITE 13	SRAHWEE OR ALTÓIR WEDGE TOMB	5 KM	
Back to Killeen cross roads. Straight ahead.			

15. Killeen Graveyard and Cross Slab
Cillín - Small Graveyard

Early Christian Church

The graveyard in Cloonlaur townland, south of Louisburgh, is widely known as Killeen. However, the original church on the site may have given its name to the neighbouring townland of Killadoon, *Cill an dúin,* "church of the fort". There is no trace of the early Christian church today but there is a circular raised platform within the old graveyard which probably indicates an enclosure within which the original church stood.

Forever Free

Storyteller James Berry recorded that the church once had *"a privilege not enjoyed by any other church in Christendom."* Tradition has it that no matter what crime a person had been found guilty of, even murder, if he escaped and ran to the church at Killeen and placed one of his fingers in the keyhole of the church door, he would be let go free.

Pagan Antiquity

In the graveyard there is a large standing stone, about 2.5m high, and leaning precariously. The stone was christianised during the seventh century when a Maltese Cross with a four-petalled tulip design, enclosed by a double circle, was incised on it.

Also in the graveyard, and marking the grave of a Reverend David Lyons, is a cross-inscribed, early Christian slab, with a main cross at the centre surrounded by four smaller crosses. This type of cross is known as the Cross of the Thieves. Markings at the bottom of the slab are obscured because of the plaque in memory of Reverend Lyons.

Pl. 35 - Standing stone with maltese cross.

Pl. 36 - Cross of the Thieves.

Reilig an Chillín agus Crosleacht

Tá an reilig seo anois sa cheantar a dtugtar an Cillín air. Mar sin féin, d'fhéadfadh sé gur thug an séipéal ar an láthair seo an t-ainm don bhaile fearainn in aice láimhe, Cill an Dúin. Níl aon rian ann den séipéal luathChríostaí ach tá ardán ciorclach sa reilig a d'fhéadfadh a bheith mar leid ar cá raibh an séipéal tráth den saol.

De réir an traidisiúin, dá gcuirfeadh duine a chiontófaí i gcoir a mhéar i bpoll na heochrach i ndoras an tséipéil ligfí saor é nó í.

Sa reilig, tá gallán cloiche mór págánach, a bhfuil leathmhaing air, agus a críostaíodh sa seachtú haois le Cros Mhálta – dearadh tiúilipe ceithredhuilleach, iata ag ciorcal dúbailte.

Tá leacht luathChríostaí mar mharc ar uaigh an Urramaigh David Lyons, agus tá príomhchros inscríofa sa lár agus ceithre chros bheaga ina timpeall. Is Cros na nGadaithe a thugtar ar an gcineál sin croise.

SITE 16	CLARE ISLAND TOWER HOUSE	13 KM + FERRY
Straight towards Louisburgh. Turn left for Roonagh Pier.		

SITE 14	BUNLAHINCH CLAPPERBRIDGE	1 KM
Left at Killeen cross roads. Straight and last right.		

Fig. viii - Clare Island Trail.
(Not to scale).

STAGE IV

Clare Island

oilean cliara

CLARE ISLAND

"The gem of the Western Isles"

The largest island in Clew Bay is Clare Island, which rises spectacularly out of the sea at the mouth of the bay. The dominating feature of the island is a ridge that runs east to west, reaching a height of 465 metres at the mountain of Knockmore or Croaghmore. The Atlantic Ocean has carved some of the steepest and highest cliffs in Ireland along the island's northern shore. These cliffs are listed as an area of international scientific importance, sheltering rare arctic-alpine plant communities and seabird breeding colonies.

Clare Island comprises 4,053 acres, is 8 km long and 5 km wide. It is nearly 6 km from the nearest mainland harbour at Roonagh (four miles west of Louisburgh) and is 30 km from Westport.

The island has a long history of habitation from at least 3,500 BC. Just before the Great Famine of the mid-1840s, Clare Island's population reached its highest, with 1,700 people. The island's landscape is still marked by the remains of tillage from this pre-famine era. Today, just over 150 people live on the island permanently, a population which swells during the summer holiday season.

First Clare Island Survey

During the years 1909 and 1911, the most ambitious natural history project ever

Pl. 37 - Winter on Clare Island.

Pl. 38 - Cliffs of the island.

undertaken in Ireland, the Clare Island Survey, was carried out by the Royal Irish Academy under the direction of Robert Lloyd Praeger. This was the first major biological survey of a specific area carried out in the world.

The data which was collected by more than 100 scientists from Ireland, Denmark, Germany, Switzerland and Britain, represented the most comprehensive inventory of nature in a single geographical location during the early part of this century.

New Survey

The island was recently surveyed again by the Royal Irish Academy. Its location on the western fringes of Europe and its pristine environment, make it a perfect baseline monitoring site. As the RIA explains *"In this period of environmental change, there is a critical need for baseline surveys in unpolluted environments, against which future changes can be measured. .... In many ways, this beautiful island is a microcosm of all that is the west of Ireland: unpolluted, yet sensitive to fundamental global changes."*

The first, second and third volumes of the survey are now available. The first volume is about the history and cultural landscape, the second volume is about the geology of the island and the third volume is about marine intertidal ecology. Future volumes will cover flora, fauna and bird life on the island.

GRANUAILE
or Grace O'Malley

The seafaring O'Malley clan of Murrisk and Clare Island rose to their height of power during the early 14th century, at a time when Gaelic chieftains throughout the west were regaining power from the flawed Anglo-Norman conquest of the area. The O'Malley coat of arms bore the Latin motto *Terra marique potens*, which translates as Powerful by land and sea. And powerful they certainly were. They ruled the southern shores of Clew Bay for over 300 years. In that time, they earned a reputation as ruthless pirates, terrorising shipping to and from Galway town. They were involved in trade between the west coast of Ireland and the coastal areas of France and particularly Spain.

Legendary Sea Captain

Pl. 39 - Statue of Granuaile at Westport House.

"There came to me also a most famous feminine sea captain called Grany Imallye, and offered her services unto me, wheresoever I would command her, with three galleys and 200 fighting men, either in Scotland or Ireland; she brought with her, her husband for she was as well by sea as by land well more than Mrs. Mate with him .... This was a notorious woman in all the coasts of Ireland."

Sir Henry Sidney, 1577
Lord Deputy of Ireland

The most famous O'Malley is Granuaile or Grace O'Malley, a name which is reputed to come from the Irish for bald (Mhaol). Legend has it that young Grainne wanted to go on a trading mission with her father, Dubhdara (Black Oak) O'Malley. However, she wasn't allowed to go because she was a girl.
So, Grainne, undeterred, shaved off her hair to disguise herself as a boy and the now "bald" Grainne managed to get on board.

Larger than Life

Legends and stories of Granuaile's exploits throughout the sixteenth century abound – some are based in fact but have been exaggerated with time and some are pure fantasy. Whether based in fact or fiction, however, the name Granuaile or Grace O'Malley, conjures up, for most, the image of a powerful, adventurous and amazon-type woman, sometimes ruthless and domineering but always courageous in her defence of Mayo.

Granuaile was born in 1530 at Belclare Castle, near Westport. At 15 she married Dónal O'Flaherty, who was a chieftain of Connemara and an ally of the O'Malleys. Her first husband was murdered and Grace then married Richard Burke in 1566. Such was her reputation, however, Richard was forever known as the husband of Granuaile.

Shortly afterwards she gave birth to a son, Tiobóid na Long, "Toby of the Ships". Legend has it that she gave birth at sea and that within a day, she was leading her ships into battle with Algerian pirates.

Rebellion, Internal Feuds andTitle

After almost 15 years of battles, upheaval, and eventually, negotiation with the English governor of Connacht, Sir Nicholas Malby in 1580, Granuaile's husband, Richard Burke, was granted a knighthood and allowed to retain the highest title in Connacht, the McWilliam title. But, his hard-won title and the couple's accompanying wealth did not last for long. Richard Burke died in 1583. Sir Nicholas Malby, who favoured the Burkes, died the next year. The Governorship of Connacht passed to Sir Richard Bingham, who believed that the *"Irish were never tamed with words but with swords."*

Granuaile was not held in high esteem by the new Governor, who claimed that she was a *"nurse to all rebellions in the province for 40 years."* The issue of rights to the McWilliam title continued to be a bone of contention between Bingham and Granuaile. This culminated in an attack on Mayo by Bingham and his army in the early 1590s. Bingham ordered a fleet of ships to attack the islands in Clew Bay, which had been used as refuges by the O'Malleys for centuries.

Audience with Queen Elizabeth I

Feeling completely persecuted by Bingham and his men, Granuaile made an historic journey to England, sailing up the Thames for an audience with Queen Elizabeth I about her plight. This equally strong woman was suitably impressed by the Irish Chieftain. She granted Granuaile pardon and ordered the release of her son and half-brother, who had been imprisoned in the meantime by Bingham. Furthermore, the Queen ordered Bingham to *"protect them to live in peace and to enjoy their livelihoods."*

Not much is known about these final years of "peace" for Granuaile. It is reputed that she died in 1603 at Rockfleet Castle on the northern coast of Clew Bay, and was buried in the Cistercian Abbey on Clare Island.

Fig. ix - O'Malley Coat of Arms.

16. Clare Island Tower House

Gleann - The Valley

The castle which commands the main harbour on Clare Island is a fine example of a Tower House, built by the O'Malleys in the 16th century.

During medieval times, the O'Malley galleys probably landed on the sandy beach nearby. Granuaile, the O'Malley Chief and Sea Captain, lived here for a while. It is said that the cable of her chief galley was passed through a hole in the wall and fastened to her bedpost, so that she might be more readily alarmed in case of an attempted attack.

Even those not intent on attack were unlikely to get a friendly reception at the Tower House.

After the defeat of the Spanish Armada a Spanish galleon sank off the shores of Clare Island with the loss of 200 lives. Less than 100 struggled ashore; and when the survivors arrived on the island most were killed by the O'Malleys from this Tower House.

There is a legend that the Tower was struck by lightening in 1750, killing a dog at the feet of the O'Malley who owned the castle, at that time. As a result he abandoned the site.

Uniquely Irish Form of Residence

Tower Houses are a form of castle built by the ruling Irish Chieftains in the 15th and early 16th centuries. They were intended to serve more as a fortified residence than a self-sufficient castle. They were often designed to a standard plan which can be seen at Clare Island: rectangular, three storeys high with a vault over the ground floor, and topped by a pitched slate or thatched roof. The roof was protected by a battlement parapet, sometimes featuring an overhang above the entrance so that objects could be dropped directly on attackers. Within the thickness of the walls were staircase passages and other features, such as garderobes (medieval lavatories).

Pl. 40 - The Tower House commands the harbour at Clare Island.

If you enter the Tower House on Clare Island, you will see that to the left of the main entrance is a passage with stone stairs beginning at first floor level. Access to these stairs may have been via a wooden staircase from the ground floor. The main living room was at first floor level and from here it was possible to access the bartizans (roofed, floorless turrets) and the garderobe.

Police Barracks

The Tower House was converted into a police barracks around 1826, when the purple slate flashing was added to the two bartizans projecting from opposite angles of the tower.

Túrtheach Chliara

Is sampla maith é an caisleán seo de thúrtheach, a thóg muintir Uí Mháille sa séú haois déag. Rinneadh túrthithe a dhearadh de réir plean caighdeánach mar a fheictear anseo: dronuilleach, trí stór ar airde agus boghta os cionn urlár na talún mar aon le slinn chlaonta nó díon ceann tuí ar a bharr. Bhí cosaint ag an díon le huchtbhalla táibhle os cionn an bhealaigh isteach ionas go bhféadfaí rudaí a chaitheamh anuas díreach ar dhaoine a bheadh ag ionsaí na háite. Bhíodh bealaí staighre agus gnéithe eile, mar losáin, nó leithris istigh sna ballaí.

Má théann tú isteach sa Túrtheach ar Chliara, feicfidh tú ar thaobh na láimhe clé de phríomhbhealach isteach pasáiste balla le staighre cloiche ag tosú ar an gcéad urlár. D'fhéadfadh sé go raibh teacht ar an staighre seo trí staighre adhmaid ó urlár na talún. Bhí an príomhsheomra cónaithe ar an gcéad urlár agus bealach uaidh go dtí na bartasáin (túiríní faoi dhíon, gan urlár) agus losán.

Tiontaíodh an Caisleán isteach ina bheairic póilíní thart ar an mbliain 1826, agus tá a fhianaise sin le feiceáil sa slinn chorcra atá ar an dá bhartasán.

SITE 17	CLARE ISLAND ABBEY	2 KM
Straight ahead. Left at beach junction. Veer right at Shop / Post Office.		

SITE 15	KILLEEN GRAVEYARD & CROSS SLAB	13 KM + FERRY
Ferry to Roonagh. Right at junction with Main Road and straight ahead.		

17. Clare Island Abbey, Kill.

Cille - The Church

Clare Island Abbey is said to date from the mid-13th century, although it was rebuilt around 1460. It was a cell of the Cistercian Abbey in Abbeyknockmoy, Co. Galway. It is currently being restored by the Office of Public Works.

The building consists simply of a nave and chancel divided by an arch. The chancel is spanned by a fine barrel vault, and a staircase in the south wall leads to the domestic chamber above the vault.

Finest Examples of Wall Paintings in Ireland

The chancel is lit by only two slender ogee-headed windows (arch over a window formed with reverse curves, giving an onion-shaped head) and must always have been dark. As a result the paintings on the ceilings and walls are among the finest examples of medieval paintings in Ireland. They have been the subject of an extensive conservation programme involving the expertise of conservators from throughout Europe. The themes of the paintings are mostly secular, offering a unique glimpse of medieval life. Scenes include a cattle raid, a knight dressed in chain mail on horseback, wolves attacking stags, musicians, dragons and griffins.

O'Malley Coat of Arms

The Abbey also houses a stone plaque with the O'Malley coat of arms, featuring a stallion surmounting a helmet, which is in turn above a boar – a symbol of warriors. The boar is surrounded by three bows with arrows pointing at it. Below the boar is an inscription with the name O'Maille (O'Malley) and the Latin motto Terra marique potens – Powerful by land and sea.

Burial Site of Granuaile

In addition, there is a canopied tomb, which is reputed to be the burial site of Grace O'Malley (although it is probably 15th century in date). It was originally painted in red, white and black. However, today, the stone used in the tomb has reverted to its grey colour.

Pl. 41 - Abbey on Clare Island.

Pl. 42 - West Gable.

Pl. 43 - A Knight dressed in chain mail on horseback, one of the Clare Island Abbey wall paintings.

Mainistir Chliara

Luaitear dáta ó lár an 13ú hAois le Mainistir Chliara, cé gur tógadh an athuair é thart ar an mbliain 1460. Ba chillín de Mhainistir Chistéirseach i Mainistir Chnoc Muaidhe, Co. na Gaillimhe a bhí ann.

Is corp agus saingeal atá san fhoirgneamh agus áirse á roinnt. Tá an saingeal á thrasnú ag boghta mín baraille, agus téann staighre sa bhalla ó dheas go dtí seomra tí os cionn an bhoghta. Níl thagann aon sholas isteach sa saingeal ach ó dhá fhuinneog chúnga ceannchíoma (áirse os cionn fuinneoige a dhéantar le cuara cúil, a thugann ceann ar chruth oinniúin) agus caithfidh go raibh an áit dorcha i gcónaí. Tá na pictiúir atá ar an tsíleáil agus ar na ballaí ar na samplaí is fearr de phictiúir mhéanaoiseacha in Éirinn. Tháinig siad faoi chlár forleathan caomhnaithe lenar bhain saineolas caomhnóirí ó ar fud na hEorpa. Is téamaí tuata is mó atá sna pictiúir, rud a thugann spléachadh uathúil dúinn ar shaol na meánaoise: Radharcanna lena n-áirítear táin bó, ridire faoi chulaith mháilleach ar muin capaill, madraí alta ag ionsaí fianna, ceoltóirí, dragain agus gríobha.

Tá plaic chloiche sa Mhainistir freisin ar a bhfuil armas Uí Mháille. Chomh maith leis sin, tá tuama forscátha ann, áit a ndeirtear go bhfuil Gráinne Uaile curtha.

SITE 18	PROMONTORY FORT	500 M
Walk in front of church. At road, turn left downhill. Cross road and continue. Cross field at sign.		

SITE 16	CLARE ISLAND TOWER HOUSE	2 KM
Back to Shop / Post Office. Veer left and straight for 2 km. Right at beach.		

18. Bronze Age Promontory Fort, Lecarrow.

Lethceathrú - The Middle Quarter

The island, like many others on the West Coast of Ireland, is edged by Promontory Forts. These forts are often some of the most dramatically located monuments on the Irish landscape.

Ancient Defensive Positions

In use from the late Bronze Age up to medieval times, Promontory Forts were defensive living areas built on top of headlands and cliffs. Their strategic location protected their inhabitants from sea invasion by the steep cliffs. A bank of earth and stones built on the landward side made attack difficult.

There are at least five Promontory Fort sites on Clare Island, a number of which include the remains of dwellings used by the defending inhabitants.

Pl. 44 - Outline of promontory fort boundary.

Dún Cinn Tíre

Bhíodh Dúnta Cinn Tíre in úsáid ó dheireadh na Cré-umhaoise go dtí an mheánaois, agus ba réimsí cosanta cónaithe iad a tógadh ar chinn tíre nó ar aillte, mar a fheictear anseo. Thug a suíomh straitéiseach mar aon leis na haillte géara cosaint do na háititheoirí ó ionradh farraige. Thógtaí carnán talún nó clocha ar thaobh na talún de ionas go mbeadh sé deacair an dún a ionsaí.

Tá ar a laghad cúig shuíomh dún cinn tíre ar Chliara, agus tá fothraigh na dtithe a bhíodh in úsáid ag na háititheoirí le fáil i roinnt acu.

SITE 19	SIGNAL TOWER, TUAR MÓR	4 KM	
Back to road. Uphill to junction. Turn left to end of road. Over fields.			

SITE 17	CLARE ISLAND ABBEY	500 M	
Back to road. Uphill and across junction. Turn right.			

19. Signal Tower, Toormore

Tuar Mór - The Big Tower

At the most western point of the Island, at Toormore, there are the ruins of a signal tower, built in 1804. Signal towers, such as this example, were built in direct response to landings by the French in Ireland in 1798 and as a defence against the threat of further such landings.

The cost and effort involved in the construction of the tower must have been exorbitant in its day and belies the strategic importance of the West of Ireland as a gateway to invading the British Empire.

The Clare Island tower is one of a line of interlinked towers along the coast. The next one to the north is on Achill Island and, to the south, on Inishturk.

Túr Comharthaíochta, Tuar Mór

Tógadh túir chomharthaíochta ar nós an sampla seo mar fhreagairt dhíreach ar na Francaigh a theacht i dtír in Éirinn sa bhliain 1798, agus ba mar chosaint iad in aghaidh an baol a bhí ann go ndéanfaí ionsaithe eile níos faide anonn. Tógadh an túr comharthaíochta seo sa bhliain 1804.

Caithfidh sé go raibh an costas agus an t-anró a bhain leis an túr a thógáil an-mhór ar fad an tráth úd agus bréagnaíonn sé an tábhacht straitéiseach a bhí le hIarthar na hÉireann mar gheata chun Impireacht na Breataine a ionsaí. Tá an túr seo ar cheann de líne de thúir idirnasctha ar feadh an chósta. Tá an chéad cheann eile ó Thuaidh de ar Acaill agus an ceann is gaire ó dheas ar Inis Toirc.

Pl. 45 - The Signal Tower was built in response to French landings.

SITE 20	MEGALITHIC TOMB	8 KM	
Back to road. Straight. Take left at beach and first left at Community Centre to first gate. Follow boundary wall to bend. At bend, walk straight across fields.			

SITE 18	PROMONTORY FORT	4 KM	
Back to road. Straight to junction before Shop / Post Office. Right. Over fields at sign.			

20. Megalithic Tomb, Porteen Finoish

Court Tomb

A megalithic court tomb can be found at Porteen Finoish, on the east side of the Island. This is one of a number of court tombs which were built along the West Coast by Neolithic farmers to bury their elite. This tomb is beautifully sited, beside a small lake, or lochán, and with a panoramic view east to Clew Bay and across to Croagh Patrick. Many tombs in the west were built facing to the east.

Court tombs were so-called because of the arrangement of stones which form an open-air court in front of the entrance to the tomb. This court area appears to reflect the communal nature of the funerary rituals and ceremonies which took place during this period. Indeed many of these tombs may also have been used as monuments for other religious ceremonies during the year.

Ancient Farming Community

The existence of the court tomb here establishes that there was a farming community on Clare Island some 5,500 years ago. Early field walls and traces of an ancient forest can be seen in the cutaway bog due north of this tomb.

Pl. 46 - The court tomb with famine landscape behind.

You will see that an ancient wall running down the nearby raised ground disappears under the lake and reappears again on the other side, indicating that the wall was in existence before the sediment lake.

Excellent traces of the famine landscape can also be seen at this site. All around are the raised potato drills used by tenant farmers to grow their staple crop.

Pl. 47 - The view east from the tomb.

Tuama Megiliteach

Tá an tuama seo ar cheann de roinnt tuamaí cúirte a thóg feirmeoirí neoiliteacha ar feadh chósta an Iarthair chun a gcuid uaisle a adhlacadh iontu.

Tugtar tuamaí cúirte orthu mar gheall ar an gcóiríocht chloch a dhéanann cúirt faoin aer os comhair an bhealaigh isteach chuig an tuama, a léiríonn b'fhéidir nádúr pobail na ndeasghnáth agus na searmanas sochraide a bhíodh ag tarlú ann.

Cruthaíonn an tuama cúirte seo go raibh pobal feirmeoireachta ar Chliara thart ar 5,500 bliain ó shin. Is féidir luathbhallaí garraithe agus rianta d'fhoraois ársa a fheiceáil sa lagphortach ó thuaidh den tuama seo. Is féidir rianta den scoth de thírdhreach ó aimsir an Ghorta a fheiceáil ag an láthair seo chomh maith. Tá iomairí fataí a bhíodh á n-úsáid ag na feirmeoirí tionóntaí lena bpríomhbharra a fhás le feiceáil ar fud na háite.

SITE 21	FULACHT FIADH	500 M
With back to tomb (east), walk straight over fields. Fulacht Fiadh in dip in line with next boundary wall.		

SITE 19	SIGNAL TOWER	8 KM
Back to road. Right at Community Centre. First right at beach and straight. Over fields.		

21. Fulacht Fiadh, Porteen Finoish

Bronze Age Cooking Sites

Fulachta Fiadh were Bronze Age open-air cooking sites which were used by the island inhabitants about 2,500 years ago. A hole in the ground was filled with water. Stones were heated on a fire and dropped into the water to bring it to boiling point. Then the meat, usually wrapped in straw, was lowered into the boiling water. Hot stones were continuously dropped into the water until the meat was cooked.

There are 53 identified fulachta fiadh on Clare Island, including some classic examples. At this site there are three in a row. These sites are generally identifiable as grass-covered horseshoe-shaped mounds, located adjacent to a small spring. They can be identified further by the presence of burnt stones in the vicinity of the cooking area.

Fulacht Fia

Ba láithreacha cócaireachta amuigh faoin aer sa Chré-Umhaois a bhí i bhFulachtaí Fia agus bhídís á n-úsáid ag na daoine a mhair ar an oileán thart ar 2,500 bliain ó shin. Líonadh poll sa talamh le huisce. Téadh clocha i dtine agus caitheadh síos san uisce iad leis an uisce a fhiuchadh. Ansin chuirtí an fheoil, le tuí casta thart uirthi de ghnáth, síos san uisce fiuchta. Chuirtí clocha te síos san uisce go seasta nó go mbeadh an fheoil bruite. Mar is léir anseo, is féidir na láithreacha seo a aithint tríd is tríd mar charnáin i gcruth crú capall clúdaithe le féar, a bhíonn suite in aice le fuarán beag. Is minic go mbíonn clocha dóite thart san áit chomh maith.

Tá 53 fulacht fiadh aitheanta ar Oileán Chliara.

Pl. 48 - Horse shoe-shaped mound with burnt stones.

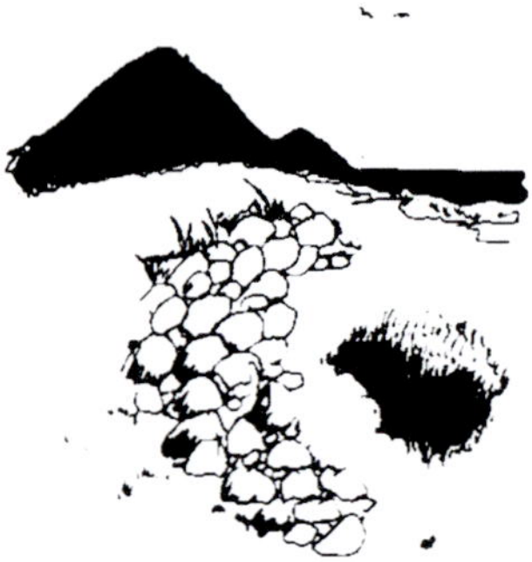

Fig. x - Fulacht Fiadh with water hole.

SITE 20	MEGALITHIC TOMB	500 KM	
With back to fulacht fiadh, walk over hillock and straight across fields. Tomb in front of small lake.			

Clew Bay Archaeological Trail Committee

The Clew Bay Trail Committee is a voluntary group made up of six local organisations including:

Croagh Patrick Archaeological Committee *(Co-ordinating only)*

Harry Hughes - *Chairman*
Gerry Walsh
Leo Morahan
Michael Gibbons
Edel Hackett

Murrisk Development Association

Johnny Groden
Eoin Campbell
Tommy Reilly
Breda Hyland

Louisburgh Community Council

Mary Fergus
Austin Francis O'Malley

Clare Island Development Company

Donal O'Shea

Westport Tourism Organisation

Bronagh Joyce
Robert Kilkelly

Westport Chamber of Commerce

Dr. Oliver Whyte

Acknowledgements

The Committee would like to acknowledge the co-operation of all of the landowners along the Trail, including:

The Office of Public Works
Westport and Louisburgh Parishes
Mayo County Council
Louisburgh Community Council
Killeen Community Council
Clare Island Commonage Landowners
Don Gibbons
Sean O'Grady
Peter McGreal
Seamus O'Toole
Bernie Winters

We would also like to thank others who helped with advice, photographs, proof reading, translation, design and encouragement, including:

Peter Hynes, Director of Services, Mayo County Council
Des Mahon, Manager, Mayo County Council
Ger Reidy, Area Engineer, Mayo County Council
South West Mayo Leader Company
Clár
Comhdháil Oileáin na hÉireann
Elizabeth Farrell
Christiaan Corlett
Aiden Clarke
Conor McKeown
John Corcoran
Europus
Ciara Cullen
The Centre for Island Studies, Clare Island
Luke Walshe
Stella Curley
Michael Gillespie
Noreen Holmes

Photographs along the Trail

Below is a list of the people who gave us permission to use their excellent photographs.

Conor McKeown, i-Contact	Front cover
Christiaan Corlett	Pls. 2, 7, 9, 20, 28, 33, 35, 36, 43.
Harry Hughes	Pls. 3, 4, 6, 13, 14, 16, 17, 18, 19.
Aiden Clarke	Pls. 12, 25, 26.
John Corcoran	Pl. 15 (entry in the Croagh Patrick Photographic Competition, 2002)

Other pictures were taken by Edel Hackett and Robert Kilkelly.

Fig. vi is a computer-generated representation of the summit of Croagh Patrick, created by Robert Kilkelly and Associates, Architects and Surveyors.

2007

Notes

(Bank Holiday)
Sunday 3/6 Roonah Point - walk S from quay along shoreline - seals basking @ low tide
Drive to south of Srulur Strand - lunch - too cold wind to stay.
Stopped at Clapperbridge then on to Silver Strand.
@ entrance to Killary Harbour.
On way back went to Srahwee megalithic slab tomb and looked at 4500yr old timbers at edge of Nahaoltra Lough.

(Bank Holiday).
Monday - 4/6. - Leckanvy Pier then Bartra Strand for most of day. walk on beach & dunes to Bartraw - the strip is the only tombola in Ireland.
Then, with difficulty located rock carvings @ Boheh.

Tuesday - 5/6. Started at Old Head - then on through Westport - to Roscahill Harbour then Claggan Quay followed causeway onto Inishnakillew drumlin.
Newport - Burrishoole Abbey - Carrickahowley Castle in Rockfleet Bay - then Furnace & Feeagh Loughs past salmon research centre - back direct
Wednesday - 6/6 lazy morning @ home!
after lunch Kilgeever Abbey @ Louisburg & then long walk on Carrowniskey Strand - north end.
Thursday 7/6. Achill Island - drove to Keem - walked up to top of Benmore Cliffs 332m - then ret. to car home via Atlantic Drive round Corraun Peninsula.

Notes

Friday 8/6. Out to Clare Island on 11am boat ret on 1pm.
Home for lunch. Then drove down to White Sand
(Sand Hills on map) - good walk on beach.

Sat 9/6 & Sun 10/6 Both days exploring headland
west of Silver Strand.

Mon. 11/6. Ballintubber Abbey, Burriscarra Friary
Lough Carra & ruins of Moore Hall

Tues 12/6 Doolough & Leenaun
Carrowmore Strand

Wed 13/6 Westport & Old Head

Thurs 14/6 Achill Island Sleivemore Deserted Village
– Trawmore Strand – Mweelin TV mast & mountain –
Dooega – Achill Sound. – direct home

Fri 15/6 Westport – W, Quay – Bertra Strand.

2008 7-21 June

Notes

Sat night Carrowmore strand - pub - dog pulled shoulder muscle!
Sun - relaxing day - dog full rest!
Mon - vet in Westport - A. did Croagh Patrick in pm.
Tues - Roonah Point to headland - seals + dolphins
Cross Strand for lunch + pm - walk to turning point in am.
Wed. (wet in pm) Bertra Strand - Westport shopping -
drumlins @ end of bay
Thurs. Silver Strand. Walk to headland - dolphins
Cross Strand on way back
Fri. Back to drumlins (Wed) - Burrishoole Abbey - drumlins
outside Mallaranny (Burrishoole) - Atlantic Drive
on south Achille to Dooega - back direct.
Sat. A + Maddy found path over to Old Head
& cliff. Carrowmore Strand then dinner
at Quay Cottage Seafood Rest.
Sun. A did Mweelrea Mtn in aft. then
all to Roonah Point - seals no dolphins!
Mon. Sites 5 + 9 to Westport. Then lunch at
Beltra Lough → Lough Conn →
Loch Cullin walk on shore → Foxford Woollen Mill
home via shops in W'port.
Tues - Roonah cliff + Bertra Strand
Wed. Village - Am. Old Head - ferry to Clare
Thurs. Strand by 'Ocean Lodge' + Silver St + head. Meal @ Quay Cottage
Fri - Westport - Bertra - Roonah Cliff.